Help Me I've Fallen

And I Can't Get Up!

T.D. JAKES

PNEUMA LIFE
PUBLISHING

Help Me I've Fallen

by T.D. Jakes

Scripture quotations in this publication, unless otherwise noted, are taken from the Holy Bible: King James Version.

Printed in the United States of America
ISBN 1-56229-435-0

Second Printing: 1995

Pneuma Life Publishing
P.O. Box 10612
Bakersfield, CA 93389-0612
(805) 324-1741

Contents

Chapter   **Page**

Introduction 4

1 What Comes Before a Fall? 5

2 In Your Darkest Hour 19

3 Getting Back on Track 33

4 Healing For Past Hurts 45

5 Strength to Stand 61

Introduction

A popular television commercial for a medical alert device featured an elderly woman who cried out, "Help! I've fallen, and I can't get up!"

The woman *wanted* to get up but couldn't. Lacking the strength to get back on her feet, she needed help.

As Christians, we all fall from time to time. Life knocks us off balance, lays us low, and renders us weak and incapacitated through no fault of our own. Something inside of us wants to stand, but we don't have the mobility or freedom to act on what we have decided to do.

The cause of the fall is not as important as what we do while we are down. Like the woman in the commercial, we must put aside fear, pride, or embarrassment and learn not only *how* to ask for help but *Whom* to ask. After all, help is just a breath away.

Chapter 1

What Comes Before a Fall?

Pride comes before destruction and a haughty spirit before a fall.

Proverbs 16:18

Pride comes before a fall. But what is pride? Pride is defined as "being high-minded; showing one's self above others." Another definition states: "Pride is a conceited sense of one's superiority." Pride has caused the fall of many great and gifted individuals.

When Self is Your God

The first known instance of pride occurred before the creation of the earth. Lucifer, the head angel in charge of praise, decided he was going to be greater than God Himself.

How art thou fallen from heaven, O Lucifer, son of the morning! how art thou cut down to the ground, which didst weaken the nations! For thou hast said in thine heart, I will ascend into heaven, I will exalt my throne above the stars of God: I will sit also upon the mount of the congregation, in the sides farthest of the north: . . . I will be like the most High (Isaiah 14:12-14).

Driven by self-deception, prideful self-delusion, and self-importance, Lucifer considered himself better than God. This explains why most of his statements begin with the word "I".

Lucifer, whose name at one time meant "light-bearer," was cast down by God to earth, where he would be known as Satan. No longer a praise leader or a majestic angel, instead he became one who roams to and fro on the earth like a lion looking for someone to devour.

Satan's pride led to his downfall. Pride and selfishness go hand in hand. Usually where there is pride, there is also the prevailing spirit of selfishness. Selfishness is defined as "loving one's self first."

Satan thought he could be better than God Himself. Of course he was wrong. Satan was deceived. How he even conceived such a thought is beyond imagination. But pride blinds us to the truth and prevents the proud from viewing life realistically.

As we know, Satan has never repented. Instead, he tries to deceive as many of God's children as possible and drag them down to share in his dreadful fallen state.

A Dangerous Place

The prophet Daniel records the downfall of the great Babylonian king, Nebuchadnezzar. One day, the king looked around at all he had accomplished and arrogantly stated: "Is not this great Babylon, that I have built for the house of the kingdom by the might of my power, and for the honour of my majesty?" (Daniel 4:30).

While he was still speaking these arrogant words, a voice from heaven said, "O King Nebuchadnezzar, to thee it is spoken; The kingdom is departed from thee" (vs. 31). That same hour, the once-great king lost his mind and began to act like an animal, eating grass until "his hairs were grown like eagles' feathers, and his nails like birds' claws" (vs. 33).

Nebuchadnezzar took his eyes off God and began to focus on his accomplishments. Forgetting *Who* had made him great, the king lost touch with reality and denied truth, thinking he was a self-made man who needed no one.

Nebuchadnezzar did not want to give God any of the glory or thanks for the growth and majesty of the kingdom. He felt that everything he owned belonged to him because he had worked for it. Sound familiar?

When put into a place of prominence, many of God's children forget who brought them to that place. This arrogant and prideful attitude has caused many to fall from the pinnacle of success and popularity.

During the 1980s, several nationally known tele-evangelists let their fame and fortune get the best of them. As a result, pride prevented them from acknowledging their need of God. Considering themselves to be beyond reproach — or advice — they let their guards down. Sin entered their lives, eventually destroying their ministries, their families, and their reputations.

When people (especially Christians who are not rooted and grounded in the Word) start acquiring prestige and experiencing monetary prosperity, they often forget that not long ago they had nothing. Before they owned a nice new car, they could barely afford to ride the bus. Before they lived in a nice new home, their family of five lived in a two-bedroom apartment, not sure how they were going to pay the rent. They were living from paycheck to paycheck.

In spite of their lack, they still managed to give God the glory whether it was by word of mouth or by giving in the offering. They knew that God would meet their needs. But once they came into a place of prosperity, they forgot it was God and God alone who blessed them. Now they look to their jobs or their businesses — or even their ministries — as their source. That is a dangerous place to be.

Contentment versus Self-Sufficiency

Where does the slippery slide into delusion begin? With discontent.

Nebuchadnezzar was not content with his increase; he wanted more. The more he was blessed, the more he wanted. His is a clear case of greed and self-sufficiency brought on by self-deception.

Deception is a trap and stronghold that ensnares many, especially those not content with their own present state in life. The Bible instructs us that we must learn to be content in whatever state we find ourselves. The apostle Paul learned that lesson well: "For I have learned, in what-soever state I am, therewith to be content" (Philippians 4:11b).

This is not to imply that we should be satisfied with being bound by the devil or be content with complacency and me-diocrity; thus, not fulfilling the call of God on our lives. Not at all. We are to work to improve ourselves while at the same time remaining totally dependent on God.

Self-sufficiency means to be "sufficient in oneself," and not putting your faith in God's assistance. Contentment, on the other hand, is to know with certainty and absolute firm conviction that God is able to meet your every need; that He, Jeho-vah, is your all sufficiency. Contentment means that you are aware that you don't covet another person's position, property, possessions, or personality. Why? Because you know and are assured that all you presently have and all that you are today is more than enough in the hands of God. Whatever you need to do to fulfill God's purpose you can do — not in your own strength — but through the strength and power of Christ that dwells within your innermost being.

The apostle Paul said, "I know both how to be abased, and I know how to abound: every where and in all things I am instructed both to be full and to be hungry, both to abound and to suffer need. I can do all things through Christ which strengtheneth me" (Philippians 4:12,13).

Where Confusion Reigns

In Nebuchadnezzar's case, the only help for him was repentance. Until he was able to look again to the Father for guidance and to recognize the Lord as his source, he was left in a world of insanity.

You may not enter into a world of insanity like Nebuchadnezzar, but the covering of God will be removed if you allow yourself to fall into an unprotected state.

If you refuse to acknowledge that you have fallen and are separated from God,

Who is the eternal source of your supply, you will find yourself in a fallen condition, unable to get up.

Like Nebuchadnezzar, you may refuse to ask for God's help. As a result, confusion will reign in your life.

Nebuchadnezzar's pride and rebellion caused him to lose his kingship until he was willing to acknowledge God.

> At the end of the days I Nebuchadnezzar lifted up mine eyes unto heaven, and mine understanding returned unto me, and I blessed the most High, and I praised and honoured him that liveth for ever . . . At the same time my reason returned unto me; . . . and I was established in my kingdom, and excellent majesty was added unto me. Now I . . . praise and extol and honour the King of heaven, all whose works are truth, and his ways judgment: and those that walk in pride he is able to abase (Daniel 4:34, 36, 37).

Repentance was the key to Nebuchadnezzar's healing and deliverance. When he acknowledged his pride and began to praise and honor God, his mind was restored. But the great king never forgot that God is able to bring low those who "walk in pride."

To fall is bad enough, but to fall and not cry out for help, refusing to repent for your sin, is worse than the fall itself. Some people are so full of pride and consumed with their own self-sufficiency that they think, "If I can't get up myself, I won't let anyone help me."

Maybe you are ashamed to let anyone know that you have fallen, because you don't want them to think less of you. It is especially difficult to ask for help if you have led people to believe that you are some great, spiritual giant, incapable of falling from your high and lofty place.

Is your image so important that you're willing to continue in your pitiful fallen state? Are you so deceived that you will not acknowledge that you have sinned? Stop being so proud. After all, isn't that what caused you to fall in the first place?

Pride is dangerous because it forces you to lie needlessly in a helpless state for days — and sometimes years. If you had asked for help immediately, you could have gotten up and gone on with your life.

The Way Back

King David began his descent into sin when he lusted for a woman who was not his wife and committed adultery. When Bathsheba became pregnant with his child, David set up her husband to be killed.

The Lord sent Nathan, the prophet of God, to reveal and convict David of his sins:

> Wherefore hast thou despised the commandment of the LORD, to do evil in his sight? thou hast killed Uriah the Hittite with the sword, and hast taken his wife to be thy wife, and hast slain him with the sword of the children of Ammon (2 Samuel 12:9).

David, realizing that God knows and sees all things, replied with great sorrow and remorse, "I have sinned against the Lord."

The Lord spared David's life, but the child that he and Bathsheba conceived died.

When David repented of his sins, God picked David up and put him back on his feet.

What if King David had not acknowledged and confessed his sins even after the prophet came to him? What if David had been so full of pride and denial that he would have allowed his kingdom to be destroyed before ever asking God for forgiveness?

Many of you are so bound by pride that you would rather let everything significant be destroyed and diminished by the devil rather than ask God for help. Some people are so prideful that they reject help even when the Lord prompts someone to give it.

We need to be more like David. When we realize we have fallen, we must repent immediately! We need to repent with urgency and sincerity as Kind David did.

Don't allow Satan to deceive you into thinking that because no one saw you commit your sin, you don't have to repent. That deception will cause you to stay in a fallen state. Don't allow pride to lock you into a state of unforgiveness.

At times, we fall and are unable to get up or even ask for help. At other times, we have fallen and just do not want to get up and try again because we are afraid we might fall again. Do not stop trying.

Like the woman in the medical alert commercial that I mentioned in the introduction, when you've fallen, scream with urgency: "Lord, help! I've fallen, and I can't get up!"

Chapter 2

In Your Darkest Hour

There is a way which seemeth right unto a man, but the end thereof are the ways of death — Proverbs 14:12.

Are you fighting against God? Maybe you have struggled in your mind, wondering: Should I ask for help? Who would be willing to help me? What if they laugh at me?

You find yourself trying to get help from everyone except God.

Giving Up the Fight

The apostle Paul, who was formerly named Saul of Tarsus, had persecuted many Christians out of religious zeal. He, too, found it hard to accept the fact that he needed help.

And as he journeyed, he came near Damascus: and suddenly there shined round about him a light from heaven: And he fell to the earth, and heard a voice saying unto him, Saul, Saul, why persecutest thou me? And he said, Who art thou, Lord? And the Lord said, I am Jesus whom thou persecutest: it is hard for thee to kick against the pricks (Acts 9:3-5).

What did Jesus mean when he said, "I am Jesus whom thou persecutest: it is hard for thee to kick against the pricks"?

The word "prick" is the King James translation for the word, "goad." Goad means "to sting; a form of aggressive agitation." Today, we say, "He tried to goad me into a fight."

In this passage from Acts, "prick" is used metaphorically to represent the prompting and pricking of the Holy Spirit that God had allowed to come upon Saul's life in an effort to get his attention. The Lord was trying to show Saul that spiritually, he was going down the wrong road and moving in a direction contrary to God's will.

Stubborn and hard-headed, Saul insisted on doing things his own way. After all, he was intelligent, capable, religious — and proud of it! As a result, it took a dramatic move of God to knock Saul off his "high horse."

After being blinded by the bright light, this radical zealot found himself in the humble position of needing someone to lead him by the hand. This temporary loss of sight was God's way of showing Saul there was Someone far greater than he.

God was saying, "Saul, why do you kick against the pricks?" In other words, "Why do you fight against what you know is true? Why do you insist on doing things your own way without first consulting Me?"

Is the Lord asking you the same question, "Why do you kick against the pricks?" The American translation puts it this way, "Why do you allow yourself to continue to run into brick walls?"

These brick walls represent sin and rebellion. Why do we continue to allow Satan to deceive us into following him? No matter how sane and rational the sin may seem to you, sin is sin.

Sin always separates us from the presence of God. What a price to pay for wanting things our own way!

In Your Time of Need

Like Saul, we sometimes find ourselves in need of not only divine but human assistance. In fact, God usually sends other people to help us in our time of need.

Blinded for three days, Saul was so depressed he couldn't eat or drink anything. At the same time that Saul thought he had reached his darkest hour, God was preparing a man named Ananias to minister to Saul.

And there was a certain disciple at Damascus, named Ananias; and to him said the Lord in a vision, Ananias. And he said, Behold, I am here, Lord. And the Lord said unto him, Arise, and go into the street which is called Straight, and inquire in the house of Judas for one called Saul, of Tarsus: for, behold, he prayeth, and hath seen in a vision a man named Ananias coming in, and putting his hand on him, that he might receive his sight . . . And Ananias went his way, and entered into the house; and putting his hands on him said, Brother Saul, the Lord, even Jesus, that appeared unto thee in the way as thou camest, hath sent me, that thou mightest receive thy sight, and be filled with the Holy Ghost. And immediately there fell from his eyes as it had been scales: and he received sight forthwith, and arose, and was baptized (Acts 9:10-12, 17, 18).

If you are in a place where you need God's divine assistance, ask the Lord to send someone to help you. There may already be people in your life who are available to bring healing and deliverance to you. You must, however, be willing to submit, as Saul did, to their ministry.

Don't fight divine connections! There is nothing to fear; God will not allow you to be hurt again.

Have you ever noticed the way zoo caretakers handle an injured animal? Even though the caretaker is only interested in helping, the animal does not understand. It only focuses on the pain and, because of this, it will strike or even kill the very person sent to help it.

Some of you may be in this very state. People who have called themselves Christians have done hurtful things to you. You did not expect them to be the ones inflicting the pain. It seemed to hurt far worse because these people professed to love the Lord.

You may have been hurt to such an extent that you no longer trust anybody, not even God. You may not have actually said, "Lord, I don't trust you," but your actions speak louder than words.

Maybe you avoid reading God's Word or refuse to allow anyone to pray for you.

Do you look for other ways to help alleviate and drown the pain?

God wants to deliver you! He wants to arrest every stronghold and every demonic spirit in your life — every demonic power, every type of sorcery, every hex, every spirit of unbelief, every spirit of doubt, every spirit of pride. God wants you set free, now!

Profile of the Fallen

What causes someone to fall? Have you experienced something so traumatic and life-changing that you have fallen away from God and forsaken the love of the Father?

Are you one of those saints who was once consumed with doing His will and only His will? Do you now haphazardly serve Him? Were you once preoccupied with spending long hours in conversation with the Lord, but you are now without time to even read His Word? Were you once consumed with the very essence of praise and worship to the Father but now opt to live without praise, except for those times of great need?

Many people fall because they are no longer grafted into the Father. They do not seek His wisdom. Without God's wisdom and the fullness of His Spirit, saints become self-deceived, self-promoting, and just plain carnal and fleshly, thinking only of self. They fool themselves into thinking they can recover by themselves without God's divine intervention or His ordained supernatural human assistance.

You've given up the fight. Deep in your inner man you have fainted in your spiritual life. You have complained about things you wanted to do but couldn't perform.

God has never said anything that He could not perform. Whether it was, "Let there be light" or "Lazarus come forth", if God said it, He always backed it up by His power and His Spirit.

Before God commissioned Moses to deliver the children of Israel out of Egyptian bondage, He first told him, "I am that I am."

If you're going to continually live a life of victory, the first thing you have got to know is that "God is able."

"He that cometh to God must believe that he is, and that he is a rewarder of them that diligently seek him" (Hebrews 11:6).

God says, "Do you not know or at least have you not heard, that I am God, the maker of heaven and earth and I change not?" In other words, God says, "There is no fainting with Me; there's no failure in Me. I AM THAT I AM."

"God resisteth the proud, but giveth grace unto the humble" (James 4:6).

When you get through searching and trying other things, you're still going to have to come back to God because He holds the power and He has your answer. It is up to you to humble yourself and say, "Lord, help! I've fallen, and I can't get up!"

Struggling in Vain

Have you been living with one foot in and one foot out of God's kingdom, giving God a "maybe," instead of "yes"? If so, it is time to stop struggling. The Holy Ghost is after you; He is in hot pursuit.

The Bible says, "At the name of Jesus every knee shall bow...And that every tongue should confess that Jesus Christ is Lord to the glory of God" (Philippians 2:10, 11). So why wait to be brought to your knees? Acknowledge Jesus as Lord of your life today. It will save you a lot of pain and sorrow.

Have ye not known? have ye not heard? hath it not been told you from the beginning? have ye not understood from the foundations of the earth?It is he that sitteth upon the circle of the earth, and the inhabitants thereof are as grasshoppers; that stretcheth out the heavens as a curtain, and spreadeth them out as a tent to dwell in: That bringeth the princes to nothing; he maketh the judges of the earth as vanity...To whom then will ye liken me, or shall I be equal? saith the Holy One. Lift up your eyes on high, and behold who hath created these things, that bringeth out their host by number: he calleth them all by names by the greatness of his might, for that he is strong in power, not one faileth. Why sayest thou, O Jacob, and speakest, O Israel, My way is hid from the Lord, and my judgment is passed over from my God? Hast thou not known? hast thou not heard, that the everlasting God, the Lord, the Creator of the ends of the earth, fainteth not, neither is weary? there is no searching of his understanding. He giveth power to the faint; and to them that have no might he increaseth strength. Even the youths shall faint and be weary, and the young men shall utterly fall: But they that wait upon the Lord shall renew their strength; they shall mount up with wings as eagles; they shall run, and not be weary; and they shall walk; and not faint (Isaiah 40:21-23, 25-31).

When your pity party is over and you are ready for His help, God will say, "Don't you know? Have you not heard who I am — the everlasting God? I am the Creator of the universe. I am not a child; I am not a school boy — I am God.

"Who do you think you're fooling? I'm God. I hold your breath in My hands. I created your body. I heat your blood just hot enough to keep you alive, but not so hot that you die. I'm God. I measured your life in the sands of my own hand. I'm God.

"Why would you serve anybody else? Who else do you allow to control your life? If it is not Me, then who? I love you. I created you in My image. I am that I am."

Why do you continue in this fallen state? What more does the Lord have to do or say to show you He loves you? Don't let Satan continue to fool you into thinking that God has forsaken you.

Stop blaming others for your mistakes. Realize and admit that there is something wrong with you. Quit being mad at everyone and stop trying to adjust the whole world to fit your circumstances.

When some folks go down, they want to lower the standard for everyone else. They want everything to fit into their world. They want to start calling wrong, right, and calling right, wrong.

Stop doing things that you know you don't have any business doing. Repent and confess your sins instead of spending your time pointing out the sins of everyone else. Admit that you have fallen so that your healing may begin.

Stop running into those brick walls. Die to your pride and ask for help! He will help you and restore you to your former state. Just ask for help. Let your heart be opened to God. He will be there for you, even in your darkest hour.

Chapter 3

Getting Back on Track

Wherefore let him that thinketh he
standeth take heed lest he fall
—1 Corinthians 10:12.

You may have heard the story about the
misbehaving little boy whose mother told
him to sit in the corner chair. "I may be
sitting on the outside," he said, "but I'm
standing on the inside."

That's the way many adults act when
they rebel against God. Standing in our
own strength, however, puts us most in
danger of falling. When we think we are
strong, we are easy prey for the devil.

Between the Devil and the Deep Blue Sea

The prophet Jonah did not want to do what he knew he was called to do. Instead, he murmured and complained and then tried to run. We can't run from God, but we can run out from the protection of the Lord.

That is what Jonah did, but God didn't stop chasing him. He caused a fish to swallow him.

While in the belly of the great fish, Jonah said, "I've messed up. I've blown it. I've goofed. I've gotten into trouble. I've gotten myself in a mess." Jonah realized he had fallen, and he was now in a place where he had to repent of his rebellion.

Then Jonah prayed unto the Lord his God out of the fish's belly, And said, I cried by reason of mine affliction unto the Lord, and he heard me; out of the belly of hell cried I, and thou heardest my voice. For thou hadst cast me into the deep, in the midst of the seas; and the

floods compassed me about: all thy
billows and thy waves passed over me.
Then I said, I am cast out of thy sight;
yet I will look again toward thy holy
temple (Jonah 2:1-4).

Notice how Jonah's emotions wavered.
At one moment, Jonah was calling on
God, but then doubt rose up in his heart
and he said, "I am cast out of God's sight."

Has the devil ever told you, "God is not
even thinking about you; God can't see
you; God doesn't love you anymore; He
doesn't care about you; after all, you
sinned"?

In the midst of Jonah's feeble prayer, the
thought popped up: "I'm too far gone, and
I'm cast out of His sight."

Have you ever had to pray with fear in
your heart and uncertainty in your spirit
not knowing in your own mind whether
God could hear you or not?

God is not deaf, nor is He hard of hear-
ing. God is not like Grandpa; He's God.
He can hear your thoughts afar off. He can

hear a snake running through the grass in the middle of a rain storm. He knows what you are trying to say even before you say it.

God will raise you up if you ask Him. Like Jonah, you don't have to do anything special to get God's attention. All He asks is that you humble yourself. God wants you delivered out of your desperate situation, but it is up to you not to resist the Holy Ghost. Submit humbly to God; resist the devil, and the devil will flee from you. First, you must submit — as Jonah did — to God and His will for your life.

Going Around in Circles

It takes more than just saying you submit to God. You have to walk it out day by day trusting Him to lead and guide you into deliverance and fulfillment. If you don't, you will only end up going around in circles.

After the children of Israel were freed from Egyptian bondage, they spent the majority of their time complaining about their circumstances. Rather than thanking God for His miraculous deliverance, they murmured and griped constantly about their living conditions.

As a result, an eleven-day journey to Canaan took forty years. The children of Israel wandered around in the wilderness until all of the original complainers died off.

> They forgat God their savior, which had done great things in Egypt; Wondrous works in the land of Ham, and terrible things by the Red sea. Therefore he said that he would destroy them, had not Moses his chosen stood before him in the breach, to turn away his wrath, lest he should destroy them. Yea, they despised the pleasant land, they believed not his word: But murmured in their tents, and hearkened not unto the voice of the LORD. Therefore he lifted up his hand against them, to overthrow them in the wilderness: To overthrow their seed also among the nations, and to scatter them in the lands (Psalm 106: 21-27).

The doubters and complainers could not enter into God's place of peace and tranquillity because of unbelief.

God had tolerated, as long as He could, the people's ungratefulness to Him for bringing them out of 400 years of hard, cruel Egyptian slavery and bondage. God had taken all He was going to of their whining and crying, like little spoiled babies, because they couldn't get their way.

He fed them meals day and night; He provided them with free lights — the sun by day and a pillar of fire by night. God put clothes on their backs and shoes on their feet, neither of which ever wore out or grew old. But through all of this, they were not content and failed to show or express to God any gratitude or thankfulness. All they did was complain, complain, and complain.

Frustrating God's Grace

The Israelites' grumbling and complaining was not what finally frustrated God's tolerance. Their immature behavior simply exemplified the condition of their hearts.

What really displeased God was their failure to walk by faith — their evil hearts of unbelief. "Take heed, brethren, lest there be in any of you an evil heart of unbelief, in departing from the living God" (Hebrews 3:12). A hard heart provokes God more than anything else.

> While it is said, Today if ye will hear his voice, harden not your hearts, as in the provocation. For some, when they had heard, did provoke: howbeit not all that came out of Egypt by Moses. But with whom was he grieved forty years? was it not with them that had sinned, whose carcases fell in the wilderness? And to whom sware he that they should not enter into his rest, but to them that believed not? (Hebrews 3:18).

When you do not trust in God's goodness and walk in unbelief, you frustrate the generous grace of God. The apostle Paul wrote, "I do not frustrate the grace of God: for if righteousness comes by the law, then Christ is dead in vain" (Galatians 2:21).

I warn you, brother and sister, do not frustrate the grace of God as the Israelites did. The Bible says that God will not always strive with man. God is merciful, longsuffering and forgiving, but that does not absolve or excuse us from yielding to the Spirit so that we may be empowered to take responsibility for our own salvation.

> Wherefore, my beloved, as ye have always obeyed, not as in my presence only, but now much more in my absence, work out your own salvation with fear and trembling. For it is God which worketh in you both to will and to do of his good pleasure (Philippians 2:12,13).

We are without excuse, for God has given us everything we need for eternal life and godliness. Why insist on doing things your own way? Submit to God and He will give you the power to overcome every obstacle in your life, one by one.

Religion can't help you. Trying to abide by legalistic church traditions won't help you out of your situation. The only source guaranteed to pull you through, every time you ask, is God Almighty.

Our Heavenly Defense Attorney

What was God's purpose for taking the Israelites through the wilderness pathway? He wanted to develop their faith in His goodness and in His ability and willingness to help them. God wanted them to know that He would care for and protect them and meet their every need regardless of the circumstances or the situations at hand.

They failed to get the picture. As a result, many were destroyed by snake bites, earthquakes, and various plagues. God would have killed them all; but Moses, who was the friend of God, gained a reprieve by pleading their case before God.

We no longer have Moses today, but as born-again citizens of the Kingdom of God, we have an Advocate who sits at the right hand of the Father constantly making intercession for the saints of Almighty God. His name is Jesus.

"Wherefore he is able also to save them to the uttermost that come unto God by him, seeing he ever liveth to make intercession for them" (Hebrews 7:25).

Before God will let you go under, He will take you over. In the meantime, you will experience "struggling time." Your faith has to be tried. And when your faith is being tested, all hell breaks loose.

During times of tribulation, demons begin to attack your faith. Satan brings false accusations against you during the trial of your faith. Principalities bring condemning indictments, but you cannot lose with the lawyer I use. Jesus has never lost a case.

The Word of God declares, "If we say that we have not sinned, we make him a liar, and his word is not in us" (1 John 1:10). But the Word of God also goes on to say that if anyone does sin, "we have an advocate with the Father, Jesus Christ the righteous" (1 John 2:1b).

Jesus Christ is our constant advocate and our high priest before God:

> Seeing then that we have a great high priest, that is passed into the heavens, Jesus the Son of God, let us hold fast our profession. For we have not an high priest which cannot be touched with the feeling of our infirmities; but was in all points tempted like as we are, yet without sin (Hebrews 4:14,15).

Do not allow your situation to lock you into a spirit of delusion and complacency. Remember, the devil is trying to kill you. He wants you dead. Only the Spirit of God and the blood of Jesus stand between you and destruction. Do not let Satan deceive you into thinking that no one cares or that God has not heard your cries for help.

God knows your moanings and your groanings. God knows what your tears mean when they well up in your eyes. If you call on Him, He will answer you.

Trust Him. If He said He will bring you through, He will.

Quit complaining about your situation. Ask God to help you, put away your pride and just ask for help. Do not allow pride to keep you immobilized in your fallen state.

Something in you has got to cry, "Lord, help! I've fallen, and I can't get up! I don't like the way I'm living; I don't like the way I'm hurting. Something in me needs to change. Something in me needs to be broken. I need to be set free by the power of God."

All you have to do is ask. God says, "Ask, and it shall be given you; seek, and ye shall find; knock, and it shall be opened unto you" (Matthew 7:7).

Remember, you have a High Priest who has made it possible for you to come boldly before the throne of grace to seek help in your time of need. When you seek God with your whole heart, you will find Him.

Chapter 4

Healing For Past Hurts

The steps of a good man are ordered by
the Lord; and he delighteth in his way.
Though he fall, he shall not be utterly
cast down: for the Lord upholdeth him
with his hand (Psalm 37:23,24).

Has something so painful and over-
whelming happened to you that it has af-
fected every area of your life? Every time
you kneel to pray, does your mind go back
to the fact that someone broke your heart
and wounded your spirit?

Have you experienced something so
personally devastating that you can't discuss it with anyone? You find it difficult
to trust people, and you don't know where
to turn. You may feel as if everyone is
grading you and evaluating your progress

— when actually you are your own harshest judge.

You know you should be further along in life, but someone or some circumstance crippled your faith. Your hopes and dreams were never fulfilled.

You know you should have finished school; you know you should have been a teacher or a musician by now. By society's standards, you should already be married and have children. Maybe you think your ministry should be further along or that you should have a successful career at this point in your life. Your dreams and goals should have been fulfilled years ago, but you've been crippled.

Don't give up. There is hope for you and healing for past hurts.

Dreams Fulfilled

Joseph had dreams. It took years, however, for those dreams to be fulfilled. In spite of the tragedies in his life, Joseph never let go of the dreams God had given him.

> Now Israel loved Joseph more than all his children, because he was the son of his old age: and he made him a coat of many colours. And when his brethren saw that their father loved him more than all his brethren, they hated him, and could not speak peaceably unto him. And Joseph dreamed a dream, and he told it his brethren: and they hated him yet the more (Genesis 37:3-5).

On the outside, Joseph was a have-not, rejected and despised by his own brothers. God had plans for Joseph long before he was ever sold into slavery. From the circumstances, however, that fact didn't always appear to be true. In the midst of many difficulties, God had His hand on Joseph's life.

While in slavery and in prison, Joseph was not experiencing conditions that indicated he was going to be successful. He didn't look like a man marked to be a great leader, but he was.

And the LORD was with Joseph, and he
was a prosperous man; and he was in
the house of his master the Egyptian.
And his master saw that the LORD was
with him, and that the LORD made all
that he did to prosper in his hand . . .
The keeper of the prison looked not to
any thing that was under his hand;
because the LORD was with him, and
that which he did, the LORD made it to
prosper (Genesis 39:2,3, 23).

God, however, has a way of taking
people who have been forsaken by men
and raising them up. In fact, God tends to
prefer such individuals because, when
they get into a place of power, they are
not arrogant like those who think they
deserve to be promoted.

Egypt's Pharaoh recognized these
qualities in Joseph and exalted him to the
highest position in the nation.

And Pharaoh said unto his servants, Can
we find such a one as this is, a man in
whom the spirit of God is? And Pharaoh
said unto Joseph, Forasmuch as God
hath shown thee all this, there is none so

discreet and wise as thou art: Thou shalt be over my house, and according unto thy word shall all my people be ruled: only in the throne will I be greater than thou. And Pharaoh said unto Joseph, See, I have set thee over all the land of Egypt (Genesis 41:38-41).

Broken individuals tend not to be quite so self-righteous. They tend to be a little warmer and more loving, reaching out to embrace others without fear of rejection. They understand that if it had not been for the Lord, they wouldn't be who they are. They realize that if it had not been for God's grace and mercy, they would have never survived.

Joseph exhibited these qualities in the way he treated his once-hateful brothers. When he revealed himself, instead of condemning them for their act of violence against him, Joseph forgave his brothers.

And Joseph said unto his brethren, Come near to me, I pray you. And they came near. And he said, I am Joseph your brother, whom ye sold into Egypt. Now

49

therefore be not grieved, nor angry with yourselves, that ye sold me hither: for God did send me before you to preserve life. For these two years hath the famine been in the land: and yet there are five years, in the which there shall neither be earing nor harvest. And God sent me before you to preserve you a posterity in the earth, and to save your lives by a great deliverance. So now it was not you that sent me hither, but God: and he hath made me a father to Pharaoh, and lord of all his house, and a ruler throughout all the land of Egypt (Genesis 45:4-8).

Joseph did not blame God for his former troubles, instead he realized that God's hand had been on his life all along.

Healed to Help Others

God has a way of bringing us out of bondage and then making us remember where we came from. When we — like Joseph — begin to experience success and victory, God will remind us that He opened the door of the prison. He set us free. He gave us favor in the eyes of men. Now it is our turn to bless others.

When God raises you up, you'll have more compassion for other people. You'll look for people you can help.

The church needs healed and delivered Christians who are willing to be used by God to bless others. God is looking for people who have enough compassion to stop and ask, "How are you today?" and then stay long enough to hear the answer.

Instead of always expecting someone to bless you, be moved to help a brother or sister in need. It was God's grace and mercy that allowed you to survive the situation that crippled you. Now it is your responsibility to remember and encourage those who may be experiencing a similar problem.

When people have been wounded and crippled by the circumstances of life, they need special care, extra attention, and un- conditional love. They have to be held a little closer and prayed over a little longer because their trust has been broken and betrayed.

They may have been told by well-meaning friends, "I'm going to be there for you." Others have said, "You can depend one me." But they lied.

I know pastors who trusted and depended on fellow associates only to be betrayed and stabbed in the back. Now these pastors are crippled and unable to minister.

I also know church people who have been disillusioned by pastors who used them and then discarded them like an old worn-out shirt. As a result, these wounded workers walk with a limp, crippled by unforgiveness and fear.

No one is exempt from being crippled, but everyone can be healed if they allow the Lord to shoulder all of their past hurts and tear down the walls of unforgiveness. Unforgiveness is a stronghold that sets up residence in the heart. It causes you to be hard-hearted, angry, and bitter toward others and even toward God!

If you forgive those who have hurt you, the Holy Spirit can bring healing. He will come to you and say, "You are hurting, but you're going to make it. You've been wounded, but I'm going to help you. I know you've got a weak side, but I'm going to strengthen you. I know you don't have a lot of help, but I'm going to be your support. I know you have been abandoned, but I'm going to stand by you."

What Only You Can Do

You may have asked "How can a perfect God have a crippled child?" God specializes in taking those who have been broken and neglected by others and restoring them. God says, "I take little and create much."

You have more potential than you think. You can achieve much more than people expect of you. You can go as far in life as your faith will take you.

They said you won't last, but He can strengthen you. They said God could not use someone like you, but He thinks differently. God sees potential that not even you know is there.

You may be saying to yourself, "I've done so much wrong, I can't get up; I'm so far out that I can't get back in."

The devil is a liar! It does not matter what you have done. It does not matter where you have been. God is a God of second chances. He is the God of new beginnings. When you're down, He'll pick you up again.

When God restores you, it does not matter who is trying to bind you or who is fighting against you. All you need to know is that when God brings you up, no demon in hell can bring you down.

If God has blessed you, shout it from the housetops! If God brought you up, praise and thank Him! Every time I think about what the Lord has done for me, my soul rejoices.

No one can tell your testimony. No one knows what God has done for you. No one knows how far you've come. No one knows what you've been through. But you know it was only by the grace of God that you survived. Don't allow the devil to steal your testimony.

It may have taken you longer than everybody else, but God has given you the victory. Tell others what God has done in your life. The devil would love for you not to tell your testimony. Why? Because if you tell what God has done for you, someone else might get set free.

God's Mercy

There is not a person alive today who has not benefitted from God's mercy. It was God's mercy that prevailed in the garden of Eden. When Adam and Eve sinned, the Lord could have scrapped everything and started all over again. God was merciful and allowed Adam and Eve to live with the hope that their seed would redeem back what they had lost.

God's mercy prevailed in the wilderness with Moses and the children of Israel. When the Israelites moaned and groaned, their fate could have ended in immediate and total destruction, but God was merciful.

When Jonah refused to go to Nineveh, God could have killed the unwilling prophet and found another to go in his place. It was God's mercy that allowed the fish to swallow Jonah. God knew what was in Jonah just as He knows what is in you and me.

Sometimes God will allow us to fall because in our time of falling we come to realize that without Him we are nothing. We become convinced that it is only by His mercy that we are able to stand.

"His mercy endureth for ever. Let the redeemed of the Lord say so" (Psalm 107:1,2). This verse reminds me of the song, "Your Grace And Mercy," which simply says:

- Your grace and mercy has brought me through,
- And I'm living this moment because of you.

- I want to thank you and praise you, too;
- Your grace and mercy has brought me through.

God's grace and mercy has brought you through. Quit acting as if you have made it on your own. Stop pretending you're here because you're so good. The devil is a liar, and he would have you deceived into thinking your deliverance was and is by some act or power of your own.

"O give thanks unto the Lord, for he is good: for his mercy endureth for ever" (Psalm 107:1).

God's Sufficient Grace

The apostle Paul wrote, "And he said unto me, My grace is sufficient for thee: for my strength is made perfect in weakness" (2 Corinthians 12:9).

When we are asking and believing God for something, it may take time for it to become a reality in our lives. As a result, the spirit of discouragement attempts to latch onto us and drag us down, saying,

"You're not going to get it. You're not going to get up. You're not going to be free. You're not going to get out. You're not going to be loosed. You're not going to be happy, and you're not going to have joy. You're not ever going to be satisfied. You're going to die frustrated. You're going to end up depressed and discouraged."

The devil is a liar. He wants us to think there is no help in God and no balm in Gilead. God may not come when you want Him to come, but He's always right on time — if you wait on Him.

"For the Lord God is a sun and shield: the Lord will give grace and glory: no good thing will he withhold from them that walk uprightly" (Psalm 84:11).

Whatever God declares or decrees, He has the power to perform. He has never yet said anything that He couldn't back up. He has never claimed to be able to do anything that He could not do.

Never be in a position where you are too good or too busy to ask God for help. Never get to a point where you think you can make it on your own. That is pride at its worst. And before a fall there is pride, and after pride there is destruction.

Without God's help, we would all be doomed to lives of pain and self-destruction. When I have been desperate and afflicted, I knew it was the power of the Holy Spirit that carried me and rescued me.

We cannot do anything without God. We can't breathe without God. We can't think without God. We can't even get up without God.

Don't let Satan deceive you into believing that you can make it on your own. As soon as you fall, Satan is right there whispering, "You will never get up."

But you can call on God for help and realize that He is always "at Hand . . . and not a God afar off" (Jeremiah 23:23).

Chapter 5

Strength to Stand

Who art thou that judgest another man's servant? to his own master he standeth or falleth. Yea, he shall be holden up: for God is able to make him stand (Romans 14:4).

Do you believe God is able to pick you up and make you stand? Until you know that God is able, you will never cry out for help.

God asked the prophet Isaiah, "Hast thou not known? hast thou not heard, that the everlasting God, the Lord, the Creator of the ends of the earth, fainteth not, neither is weary?" (Isaiah 40:28a).

God wants us to understand that there is no lack of strength in Him. You may not have much of a prayer life, but God says,

"Has thou not known?" In other words, you should have known that He would take care of you.

The Word says that the everlasting God, the Creator of the universe, is all powerful. He has brought you through many problems, so don't let Satan deceive you into thinking that it was just luck or coincidence that delivered you.

Remember what God has done for you. If you can't seem to remember anything He has done for you personally, then look around at others who have been delivered out of situations worse than yours. See what God did for them and tell yourself, "If He can do it for them, I know He can do it for me." God's divine love and power brought them through, and He will do the same for you.

God says, "I have the strength that is necessary to escalate and motivate and move you up and out of your circumstances."

What makes you think your circumstance is beyond His ability? What causes you to believe that you can't get up when God is always willing to help you back on your feet? What is it that has brought you to the place in your confession that you declare weakness greater than the strength you profess to have?

The victorious declare, "O my God, I trust in thee: let me not be ashamed, let not mine enemies triumph over me" (Psalm 25:2). Everyone who puts his trust in God overcomes because there is no limit to God's resources. God is omnipotent — all powerful.

If God has His eyes on the sparrow and has numbered the hairs on your head, you can be assured that He knows the way that you need to take in times of trouble. When it's all over, you will come forth as pure gold. God wants to show you — even more than your desire to know —that He is able to save to the uttermost.

God is strong in power, and He cannot fail. God is not only all powerful, He is also the one and only Almighty. This makes Him well able to perform whatever He has spoken.

Learning to Lean

Many Christians go through life as born again citizens of the kingdom of God yet live defeated and unfulfilled lives, having no purpose or meaning.

Why is that? Because even though they have been born again by the grace of God and blood of Jesus, they have yet to submit their lives to the Lordship of Jesus Christ. They insist on doing things their way rather than yielding to the will of God for their lives.

Such Christians refuse to take advice and cannot be told anything. They may like the pastor's preaching and may even give generously to the church, but when it comes to God altering their snug and comfortable lifestyle for the Kingdom of God, they balk. They prefer to lean on their own understanding subconsciously thinking they are smarter than God.

They live in rebellion against God's Word, which clearly commands, "Trust in the Lord with all thine heart; and lean not unto thine own understanding. In all thy ways acknowledge him, and he shall direct thy paths" (Proverbs 3:5,6).

Because of their pride, such people never seek God's counsel on anything or consult the advice of the Word of God on important decisions. When they do go to the Bible about some matter or pressing issue, they misinterpret God's Word to make it mean what they want it to say. They have become very skilled and crafty at erroneously using the Word to rationalize and justify their own selfish motivations.

Remember, "There is a way which seemeth right unto a man, but the end thereof are the ways of death" (Proverbs 14:12).

Instead of traveling this road of destruction, you can take the righteous alternative, which is the counsel of God. If you want to be victorious in all your endeavors, then don't lean on your own under-standing or to your own devices or inno-vations. Instead, in all your ways ac-knowledge the Lord, and He will direct your path.

Seek the Word of the Lord about every-thing that concerns you, and you will, like the great warrior Joshua, have good suc-cess.

If you want to be profitable in business and successful in life, develop an attitude and habit of inquiring of the Lord and you will never fail. Turn from the wicked way of your own fleshly wisdom and acknowl-edge the Lord – and He will direct your path. "For as many as are led by the Spirit of God, they are the sons of God" (Romans 8:14).

Renewed Strength

The Bible says that God "giveth power to the faint; and to them that have no might he increaseth strength" (Isaiah 40:29). In other words, He is saying, "I won't kill you because you fainted. I give power to the faint."

When you start losing the strength you once had, you are fainting. When you can hardly stand up, and you begin to stagger in the throws of sin, lust, envy, and strife, God declares, "I give power to the faint!"

God says, "I give power, not to the person who is standing strong, but to the one who is swaying on wobbly knees. I give power to the faint." To those who have no might, He said, "I will increase their strength."

If you have looked inside yourself and cannot muster the strength to get up, God says, "I will increase your strength."

Think back for a moment to the elderly woman in that commercial. She did not only need someone to help her up, but she needed someone or something to make her stronger.

God will not only raise you up, but He'll give you enough power to pull yourself up if you stumble again. He won't help you up so you can be handicapped the rest of your life. No. He gives power to the faint, and to those who are weak He gives strength.

Are you weak with no will-power, no strength, no ability within yourself to resist the enemy? When your body gets tired, remember God and His strength. When Satan begins to attack you, remember the power of God residing within your innermost being. Remember that God does not faint or grow weary. In fact, the Holy One does not even sleep.

When you remember these things about your Father, your strength will suddenly be renewed. Your joy will be restored, and your power will return. You will begin to experience a life of victory.

Waiting on God

God says, "If you wait on Me, I'll renew your strength. If you wait on Me, everything will be all right."

You may be hurt right now, but be patient. Help is on the way.

I know you've cried out, "Lord, help! I've fallen, and I can't get up." The Holy Spirit says, "Wait. Help is on the way. Just hold on, God is coming to your aid. He's coming to deliver you and to set you free."

God is going to bring you out and loose you from your captivity. He's going to renew your strength. If you hold on a little while longer, your change is going to come.

Remember Samson who lost everything; he lost his hair, his strength, and his eyes. Samson lost his position, his family, his wife, and his reputation. He was reduced from a great warrior to grinding at the mill. But without a doubt, at an appointed time, Samson's strength was renewed.

Samson's attitude was, "Lord, I'm waiting on you. If you don't help me, I'll die without ever being redeemed from the error of my ways. Lord, if you don't help me, I'll never get my honor back. God, if you don't help me, I'll never get up from where I've fallen."

While he was waiting, Samson's strength began to return.

The secret to renewing your strength is waiting on the Lord. God's Word says, "But they that wait upon the Lord shall renew their strength" (Isaiah 40:31a).

At times you may not have been able to explain it or prove it, but you knew you were waiting on something to happen in your life. The devil said, "You need to give up and die," but something inside you said, "Hold out a little while longer."

The devil said, "You're not going to get it," but something else said, "Wait. You're hurting, but wait; you're crying, but wait; you've missed it, but wait on the Lord and everything is going to be all right."

On Eagles' Wings

"They shall mount up on wings as eagles; they shall run, and not be weary;

and they shall walk, and not faint" (Isaiah 40:31b).

God declares, "I'll cause your wings to stretch out. You will mount up on wings like eagles. I'll take you above the top of the storm clouds."

The eagle does not fly *in* the storm; it flies *above* the storm. Spreading its wings wide, the eagle uses the wind blowing against it to take it higher instead of lower.

You don't have to let the wind bring you down. If you just stretch out on God's Word, the same wind that is trying to take you under will hold you up and take you over into the glory of God.

You're going to walk and not faint, but first you must come to God with your whole heart. Humble yourself and tell the Lord that you're unable to do it alone. Tell the Lord that you've tried, but you can't seem to get the victory — you just can't get up.

"Lord, I've been lying here on the ground of adversity and defeat. I've tried, but I can't get up. The desire is there in my mind and my will, but when I try to get back on my feet, I can't get my flesh to cooperate with what the Word of God says I can do. I'm thinking right, but I'm not doing right. I'm saying the right things, but I can't get up."

It is at this point that you must call out: "Lord, you've got to help me, or I'll never get out of this. Lord, help! I've fallen, and I can't get up! I'm pretending to be stronger than I am, but I need You to renew my strength. God, give me back my will to fight."

You also need to confess: "Lord, I know I'm allowing things in my life that should not be there. I repent of my sin. I want to be delivered, but I continue to be bound. I don't have the strength to deliver myself. I need the Holy Spirit working in my life again."

Brothers and sisters, when your situation gets desperate, you need to run to God like you have never run before and cry out: "Jesus, I'm on the verge of destruction. If you don't help me, the enemy is going to annihilate me. He's about to take me out! Help me, Lord Jesus!"

The Holy Spirit is calling you. Put away the excuses and the complaints. God is calling you. Give Him everything, and allow Him to renew your strength.

The areas of your life that you have not given up to Him, you need to release right now. Don't be bound any longer. The Lord will not renew your strength until you are willing to throw everything on the altar, without restrictions or reservations.

When you've given Him all of you, He'll give you all of Him – no more "some" of you and "some" of Him. It's time in your life that it's "none" of you and "all" of Him.

When you make that decision, He'll enable you to mount up on eagle's wings and soar with the mighty wind of the Spirit.

God will pick you up and make you stand.

Water in the Wilderness

God's Provision For Your Every Need

by T.D. Jakes

Just before you apprehend your greatest conquest, expect the greatest struggle. Many are perplexed who encounter this season of adversity.

This book will show you how to survive the worst of times with the greatest of ease and will cause fountains of living water to spring out of the parched, sun–drenched areas in your life. This word is a refreshing stream in the desert for the weary traveler.

To order toll free call:
T.D. Jakes Ministries
1-800-BISHOP-2

Book

Why?

Because You Are Anointed

by T.D. Jakes

Why do the righteous, who have committed their entire lives to obeying God, seem to endure so much pain and experience such conflict? These perplexing questions have plagued and bewildered Christians for ages. In this anointed and inspirational new book, Bishop T.D. Jakes, the preacher with the velvet touch and explosive delivery, provocatively and skillfully answers these questions and many more as well as answering the "Why" of the anointed.

Use order form to order directly from: T.D. Jakes Ministries

Book

Woman , Thou Art Loosed
by T.D. Jakes

This book offers healing to hurting single-mothers, insecure women, and battered wives. Abused girls and women in crises are exchanging their despair for hope! Hurting women around the nation and those who minister to them are devouring the compassionate truths in Bishop T.D. Jakes' *Woman, Thou Art Loosed.*
Also available as a workbook

Book

Can You Stand to Be Blessed?
by T.D. Jakes

Does any runner enter a race without training for it? Does a farmer expect a harvest without preparing a field? Do Christians believe they can hit the mark without taking aim?

In this book T.D. Jakes teaches you how to unlock the inner strength to go on in God. These practical scriptural principles will release you to fulfill your intended purpose. The only question that remains is, *Can You Stand to Be Blessed*?

**Use order form to
order directly from:
T.D. Jakes Ministries**

Video

MANPOWER

Healing the Wounded Man Within

Wounded men will experience the transforming power of God's Word in *Manpower*. Satan has plotted to destroy the male, but God will literally raise up thousands of men through this life-changing, soul-cleansing, and mind-renewing word. This four-part audio series is for every man who ever had an issue he could not discuss; for every man who needed to bare his heart and had no one to hear it.

To order toll free call:
T.D. Jakes Ministries
1-800-BISHOP-2

Video

GET IN THE BIRTH POSITION

Inducing Your God-Inspired Dreams

God's Word is steadfast. Nothing can stop what God has promised from coming to pass. However, you need to get ready. In this message T.D. Jakes shares the steps necessary to bring to birth the promises of God in your life.

**Use order form to
order directly from:
T.D. Jakes Ministries**

THE 25TH HOUR

When God Stops Time For You!

Have you ever thought, "Lord, I need more time?" Joshua thought the same thing, and he called upon the sun and moon to stand still! This message from Joshua 10 testifies of the mightiness of our God, who can stop time and allow His children to accomplish His purposes and realize the victory!

THE PUPPET MASTER

The vastness of God, His omnipotence and omni-presence, His working in the spirit world - these are concepts difficult to grasp. In this anointed message, T.D. Jakes declares God's ability to work for your deliverance, for He can go where you cannot go, do what you cannot do, and reach what you cannot reach!

**Use order form to
order directly from:
T.D. Jakes Ministries**

Video

RECLAIMING THE LOST ONES

TELL THE DEVIL
"I CHANGED MY MIND!"

The scriptures declare that it is with the mind that we serve the Lord. If there was ever a battleground that Satan wants to seize and dominate in your life, it's right in the arsenals of your own mind. We must get the victory in our thought-life.

I believe that even now God is calling every prodigal son back home. Both the lost and the lukewarm are being covered and clothed with His righteousness and grace. I pray that this life-changing, soul-cleansing, mind-renewing message will help you find your way from the pit back to the palace.

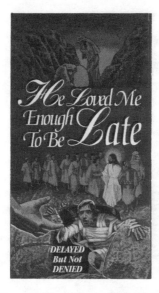

Video

HE LOVED ME ENOUGH
TO BE LATE

Delayed But Not Denied

Many of us have wondered, "God, what is taking You so long?" Often God doesn't do what we think He will, when we think He will, because He loves us. His love is willing to be criticized to accomplish its purpose. Jesus chose to wait until Lazarus had been dead four days, and still raised him up! This message will challenge you to roll away your doubt and receive your miracle from the tomb!

**Use order form to
order directly from:
T.D. Jakes Ministries**

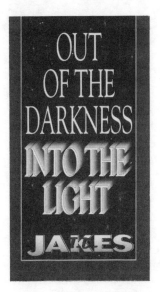

Video

OUT OF THE DARKNESS
INTO THE LIGHT

When Jesus healed a blind man on the Sabbath by putting mud on his eyes and telling him to wash, He broke tradition in favor of deliverance. The Church must follow this example. Are we willing to move with God beyond some of the things we have come from? Can we look beyond our personal dark moments to God? The Light of the world is ready to burst into our lives!

To order toll free call:
T.D. Jakes Ministries
1-800-BISHOP-2

Cassettes, Books and Videos
from
T.D. Jakes

Books

Why?
Water in the Wilderness
Help Me I've Fallen
Woman Thou Art Loosed
Can You Stand to Be Blessed?

Cassettes Series

The Gates of Hell	$20.00
Lord Save Our House	$20.00
When Helping You is Hurting Me	$20.00
Woman Thou Art Loosed (Pt 1)	$20.00
Woman Thou Art Loosed (Pt 2)	$20.00
Loose That Man & Let Him Go (Pt 1)	$20.00
Loose That Man & Let Him Go (Pt 2)	$20.00
MANPOWER: *Healing The Wounded Man Within*	
	$20.00

Video

First Lady	$20.00
Give The Man What He Wants	$20.00
The Spell Is Broken	$20.00
Turning Pressure into Power	$20.00

Audio	Video
Woman Thou Art Loosed (Azusa '93)	
$6.00	$20.00
Get in The Birth Position	
$6.00	$20.00
The 25th Hour	
$6.00	$20.00

	Audio	Video
The Puppet Master	$6.00	$20.00
Desert Babies	$6.00	$20.00
He Loved Me Enough To Be Late	$6.00	$20.00
Out Of The Darkness Into The Light	$6.00	$20.00
Tell The Devil I Changed My Mind	$6.00	$20.00
I Am Still In His Hands	$6.00	$20.00
The Kingdom Is Going To The Dogs	$6.00	$20.00

MANPOWER: *Healing The Wounded Man Within*
(4 Videos) $60.00

Hidden Mysteries Of The Cross
(12 Audio Cassettes and Home Study Workbook)
                                                   $75.00

"Woman Thou Art Loosed" Care pack
(3 Videos, 8 Audios, & 1 Book) $99.00

To Order Call Toll Free:

1-800-Bishop-2

Ordering Information

Shipping and Handling: $ 3.95
Overnight Shipments Add: $15
  Please Consider a Love Gift to the Ministry.

Credit Cards Accepted:

- ❏ Visa
- ❏ Mastercard
- ❏ American Express
- ❏ Discover

Card#: _____

Exp. Date: _____

Signature: _____

T.D. Jakes Ministries
P.O. Box 7056
Charleston, WV 25356
1-800-Bishop-2 (247-4672)

This word is a refreshing stream in the desert for the weary traveler.

When Shepherds Bleed
by T.D. Jakes

Shepherding is a dangerous profession, and no one knows that better than pastor. Drawing from personal encounters with actual shepherds in Israel and years of ministry, Bishop T.D. Jakes and Stanley Miller provide unique insight into the hazards faced by pastors today. With amazing perception, the author pull back the bandages and uncover the open, bleeding wounds common among those shepherding God's flock. Using the skills of spiritual surgeons, they precisely cut to the heart of the problem and tenderly apply the cure. You'll be moved to tears as your healing process begins. Open your heart and let God lead you beside the still waters where He can restore your soul.

The Harvest
by T.D. Jakes

Have you been sidetracked by Satan? Are you preoccupied with the things of this world? Are you distracted by one crisis after another? You need to get your act together before it's too late! God's strategy for the end-time harvest is already set in motion. Phase One is underway, and Phase Two is close behind. If you don't want to be left out tomorrow, you need to take action today. With startling insight, T.D. Jakes sets the record straight. You'll be shocked to learn how God is separating people into two distinct categories. One thing is certain – after reading *The Harvest,* you'll know exactly where you stand with God. This book will help you discover who will and who won't be included in the final ingathering and determine what it takes to be

1 - 8 0 0 - 7 2 7 - 3 2 1 8

prepared. If you miss *The Harvest,* you'll regret it for all eternity!

Becoming A Leader
by Myles Munroe

Many consider leadership to be no more than staying ahead of the pack, but that is a far cry from what leadership is. Leadership is deploying others to become as good as or better than you are. Within each of us lies the potential to be an effective leader. *Becoming A Leader* uncovers the secrets of dynamic leadership that will show you how to be a leader in your family, school, community, church and job. No matter where you are or what you do in life this book can help you to inevitably become a leader. Remember: it is never too late to become a leader. As in every tree there is a forest, so in every follower there is a leader.

Becoming A Leader Workbook
by Myles Munroe

Now you can activate your leadership potential through the *Becoming A Leader Workbook.* This workbook has been designed to take you step by step through the leadership principles taught in *Becoming A Leader.* As you participate in the work studies you will see the true leader inside you develop and grow into maturity. "***Knowledge with action produces results.***"

This is My Story
by Candi Staton

This is My Story is a touching autobiography about a gifted young child who rose from obscurity and poverty to stardom and wealth. With a music career that included selling millions of albums and topping the charts came a life of brokenness, loneliness, and de-

1 - 8 0 0 - 7 2 7 - 3 2 1 8

spair. This book will make you cry and laugh as you witness one woman's search for success and love.

The God Factor
by James Giles

Is something missing in your life? Do you find yourself at the mercy of your circumstances? Is your self-esteem at an all-time low? Are your dreams only a faded memory? You could be missing the one element that could make the difference between success and failure, poverty and prosperity, and creativity and apathy. Knowing God supplies the creative genius you need to reach your potential and realize your dream. You'll be challenged as James Giles shows you how to tap into your God-given genius, take steps toward reaching your goal, pray big and get answers, eat right and stay healthy, prosper economically and personally, and leave a lasting legacy for your children.

Making the Most of Your Teenage Years
by David Burrows

Most teenagers live for today. Living only for today, however, can kill you. When teenagers have no plan for their future, they follow a plan that someone else devised. Unfortunately, this plan often leads them to drugs, sex, crime, jail, and an early death. How can you make the most of your teenage years? Discover who you really are – and how to plan for the three phases of your life. You can develop your skill, achieve your dreams, and still have fun.

Five Years To Life
by Sam Huddleston

"One day in jail, Sam's life changed. Jesus used my daddy, not to scare the hell out of me, but to love it out of me." *Five Years To Life* is the moving account of the

1 - 8 0 0 - 7 2 7 - 3 2 1 8

power of unconditional love from an earthly father and from the heavenly Father. It's the story of a man who learned to make right choices because his heart had been dramatically changed.

The Biblical Principles of Success
Arthur L. Mackey Jr.

There are only three types of people in the world: 1) People who make things happen, 2) People who watch things happen, and 3) People who do not know what in the world is happening. *The Biblical Principles of Success* will help you become one who makes things happen. Success is not a matter of "doing it my way." It is turning from a personal, selfish philosophy to God's outreaching, sharing way of life. This powerful book teaches you how to tap into success principles that are guaranteed – *the Biblical principles of success!*

Flaming Sword
by Tai Ikomi

Scripture memorization and meditation bring tremendous spiritual power, however many Christians find it to be an uphill task. Committing Scriptures to memory will transform the mediocre Christian to a spiritual giant. This book will help you to become addicted to the powerful practice of Scripture memorization and help you obtain the victory that you desire in every area of your life. *Flaming Sword* is your pathway to spiritual growth and a more intimate relationship with God.

Four Laws of Productivity
by Dr. Mensa Otabil

Success has no favorites, but it does have associates. Success will come to anyone who will pay the price to receive its benefits. *Four Laws of Productivity* will give you the powerful keys that will help you achieve

1 - 8 0 0 - 7 2 7 - 3 2 1 8

your life's goals. You will learn how to discover God's gift in you, develop your gift, perfect your gift, and utilize your gift to its maximum potential. The principles revealed in this timely book will radically change your life.

Leadership in the New Testament Church
by Earl D. Johnson
Leadership in the New Testament Church offers practical and applicable insight into the role of leadership in the present day church. In this book, the author explains the qualities that leaders must have, explores the interpersonal relationships between the leader and his staff, the leader's influence in the church and society and how to handle conflicts that arise among leaders.

The Call of God
by Jefferson Edwards
Since I have been called to preach, now what? Many sincere Christians are confused about their call to the ministry. Some are zealous and run ahead of their time and season of training and preparation while others are behind their time neglecting the gift of God within them. *The Call of God* gives practical instruction for pastors and leaders to refine and further develop their ministry and tips on how to nourish and develop others with God's call to effectively proclaim the gospel of Christ. *The Call of God* will help you to • Have clarity from God as to what ministry involves • Be able to identify and affirm the call in your life • See what stage you are in your call from God • Remove confusion in relation to the processing of a call or the making of the person • Understand the development of the anointing to fulfill your call.

1 - 8 0 0 - 7 2 7 - 3 2 1 8

The Layman's Guide to Counseling
by Susan Wallace

The increasing need for counseling has caused today's Christian leaders to become more sensitive to raise up lay-counselors to share this burden with them. Jesus' command is to "set the captives free." *The Layman's Guide to Counseling* shows you how. A number of visual aids in the form of charts, lists, and tables are also integrated into this reference book: the most comprehensive counseling tool available. *The Layman's Guide to Counseling* gives you the knowledge you need to use advanced principles of Word-based counseling to equip you to be effective in your counseling ministry. **Topics Include** • Inner Healing • Parenting • Marriage • Deliverance • Abuse • Forgiveness • Drug & Alcohol Recovery • Youth Counseling • Holy Spirit • Premarital Counseling

The Church
by Turnel Nelson

Discover God's true intent and purpose for His Church in this powerful new release by Pastor Turnel Nelson. This book speaks to the individual with an exciting freshness and urgency to become the true Bride of Christ.

Another Look at Sex
by Charles Phillips

This book is undoubtedly a head turner and eye opener that will cause you to take another close look at sex. In this book, Charles Phillips openly addresses this seldom discussed subject and gives life-changing advice on sex to married couples and singles. If you have questions about sex, this is the book for you.

1 - 8 0 0 - 7 2 7 - 3 2 1 8

The Believer's Topical Bible
by Derwin Stewart

The Believer's Topical Bible covers every aspect of a Christian's relationship with God and man, providing biblical answers and solutions for many challenges. It is a quick, convenient, and thorough reference Bible that has been designed for use in personal devotions and group Bible studies. With over 3,800 verses systematically organized under 240 topics, it is the largest devotional-topical Bible available in the New International Version and the King James Version.

Available at your local bookstore or by contacting:

Pneuma Life Publishing
P.O. Box 10612
Bakersfield, CA 93389-0612

1-800-727-3218
1-805-324-1741